TADHG CULLEY

'Shards Of A Ceramic Soul:
A Poetry Chapbook'
Copyright © Tadhg Culley 2021.
Cover Image by Tima Miroshnichencko from Pexels

Contact the author at:
undotheheartbreak@gmail.com

ISBN: 9798467404356

Copyright Notice: All rights reserved. Without limiting the rights under copyright reserved above, no part of this publication may be reproduced, stored in or introduced into a retrieval system, or transmitted, in any form, or by any means (electronic, mechanical, photocopying, recording, or otherwise) without the prior written permission of the copyright owner of this book, except for brief quotations embodied in critical reviews and certain other non-commercial uses permitted by copyright law.

SHARDS OF A CERAMIC SOUL

'Broken But Ne'er Undone'

What causes me, with broken back,
To slump o'er a typewriter?
To hammer at the keys of letters,
To ask to tighten my own rack...

What causes me, with shattered knee,
To dream of times gone by?
Athletic yearnings stir my soul,
When youth has long departed.

What causes me, with cracked ribs,
To conjure up a fiction?
One where I came out the victor,
In all the losses I know too well.

What causes me, with bent fingers,
To wrap the hands in gloves?
To think of one time I'd return,
To that ring I left behind.

What causes me, with ailing mind,
To dream and nightmare of a time,
Long left behind?
In *all* of my imaginings.

What causes me, with tortured heart,
To rise up once again?
Into love's fierce arena,
To say: "I'll love again".

What causes me, with scarred skin,
To dare to venture back?
To that which once had ruined me,
To risk one more fatal injury...

TADHG CULLEY

What causes me, with failure's list,
To yet but strive once more?
To think that better circumstance,
Might be waiting behind that door.

What causes me, with fading memory,
To arrange these words again?
To write about a life gone by,
With unknown future pending...

I'll tell you one thing I *might* know,
To try to answer this.
(Yet I declare how "I *know*,
"That I know *nothing*"...)

Still, I'll try to say,
That of these few questions,
(With so many more unasked):
It's only that I do not know

how to quit.

SHARDS OF A CERAMIC SOUL

'How?'

How can I be forgotten,
If I was never known?
How can I ever lose a thing,
If I have owned nothing?

How can I e'er be mourned,
If I'd not yet lived life?
How can I have known real grief,
If I never knew total love?

How can I ever die,
If my life was naught but dream?
How can I ever live,
If we are born to learn we'll die?

How can I even sing,
If I have no audience?
How can I ever dance,
If I share no dalliance?

How can I dare to speak,
If I have no-one to listen?
How can I feign to shout,
If I breathe for limited time?

How can I dream to write,
If I have no fans to read?
How can I hope to dream,
If I beat on broken heart?

How can I learn to love,
If I can suffer no more loss?
How can I live alone,
If I yearn for real connection?

TADHG CULLEY

How can I fill the pages,
If I know books can be burnt?
How can I print the tomes,
If I have no-one to buy them?

How can I breathe in again,
If I must but breathe out after?
How can I pick up pen,
If I only know rejection?

How can I go on living,
If I only see destruction?
How can I bear the heartache,
If I can't bear lost affection?

How can I think of death,
If I have only known this life?
How can I ask a question,
If I never find one answer?

'Breadcrumb Remains'

What remains of human life,
But the fumes of a spent soul?
Where burns the body, used as coal,
Breaking to melting point our minds.

Is the remnant of existence,
A single independent source?
Will we return all that was borrowed?
Do unspent dreams make our hearts hollow?

Carve out a corner of this Earth,
To spend your years within a tomb,
To bargain Fate and capture Fame,
Then realize you are *not* saved...

The moment's gone; all memories lost;
Life flew by but at what cost?
Did you pursue your truthful path?
Did you attain what you came for?

The decades go, roll on and on...
If Time existed, it flies by,
If flight existed, it was time!
We can but follow:

the breadcrumbs of a life...

TADHG CULLEY

'Cave Dwelling'

Having hidden in a cave,
During my bountiful years,
Heaven-sent prophecies,
Found me forming only tears.

Light that shone from out of heart,
Came to darken the decay,
Illuminating ancient ways;
Where Poets pray to Prophet's ears.

In that cave, all Fear amassed,
Spiders, spectres, spirits, sprites,
Came to kill all that ignites,
My hope, my heart, my soul; my *mass*.

There, while hiding in that cave,
Torture wracked my back anew,
Cracked and tacked and hacked and sacked,
Black misery was beaten blue.

Then, emerging from that cave,
They'd not yet snuffed out dimming light,
There, contrite, my eyes saw sights,
That gave new life to feeble rays.

Shining with a dying power,
Served to soften final hour,
Shone to silence angry ghosts,
Spreading 'round the entire globe.

Gave fresh time to hope reborn,
To tell a tale of a tomb scorned.

'Descend Sweet Muse'

As the Muse descends,
Life itself can bend,
Painting out in thought,
Memories *she* wrought.

Human-being device,
While dreaming of flight,
Serves to channel words,
To share with the herds.

Here we cannot reach,
Destinations breached,
Here we can but write,
Poetry at night.

As the Muse descends,
Life itself can bend,
Painting out in thought,
Memories *he* caught.

TADHG CULLEY

'Hubris Is The Fashion Of The Times'

I notice a disturbing pattern,
Forming a societal trend,
Where every man calls himself a King,
Where every woman calls herself a Queen.

With no dynastic heritage,
With no regal bloodline,
No coat of arms nor latin motto,
No nation to serve nor rule.

No throne to call their home,
No crown to dress their skulls,
No royalty to speak of,
Except self-made delusion...

So many see themselves,
As living, walking Gods/Goddesses,
Here comes the Master, Meet the Mistress;
Their self-love morphs into hubris.

Titles once earnt now self-appointed,
As if the latest flowery scarf to wear,
With no knowledge of ancestral history,
Yet they claim the bounty of the world.

Here, meet the King of his own Umbrage,
Now, meet the Queen of her own Ego,
There, meet Lord of his own Masturbation,
Then, meet Lady of her own Deception.

Their one true Mastery? THE SELFIE!
Without wise tutelage to speak of,
They claim the planet as being their birthright,
With demands as lofty as their narcissism.

These skill-less, fruitless, hollow forms,
Commanding views in the billions,
Subscribership in the millions,
Share not one thing of value with their sheep.

Not one real gift to offer humanity,
Except selling their clothes and make-up lines,
Served by serving their own made-up lies,
In fact, they lower posterity; for one and all.

TADHG CULLEY

'Short-Term Loss'

My memory is oh so bad,
I often e'en forget myself,
Losing shards of ceramic soul,
Forgetting why I've come to Earth.

As if my fading memory,
Or my growing beard,
Or my grey-flecked hair,
Spoke of time-lost perplexity.

If we can forget ourselves,
Are our lives confined to thought?
As if the numbered days and years,
Were but the *idea* of someone's life.

What can make the memory whole?
If life is never constant.
It can't be captured, won't be bought,
Never stands still, can't be caught.

We face our own mortality,
With each breath; breathe in and out.
In and out, like our shore-lives,
Had only Death to e'er call sure.

Our end is the one guarantee,
That comes with life. So sad but true,
Perhaps this short-term memory loss,
Gives rare glimpse at what death must be like.

'Sometimes (Most Times) Mending Heartbreak'

Sometimes I wish I had never met her,
Was a few years' worth of love,
Worth this much wasted energy?
We met almost two decades ago,
We broke up o'er seven years ago,
Our time together? Two years, three months...
Our time apart is nearly thrice that!
And yet she does not leave,
My mind, body, heart, life, soul.
Why will she not simply go?
No matter how hard I beg her to leave,
My memory. Yet still she lingers there.
It's not her fault. Nor is it mine.
In that time since we parted, she left and I lived on.
I've had a longer love of four years, since.
And while that ended a mere two years ago,
I'm over that already... *(I don't say that to be cruel.*
I've mourned, grieved, healed, moved on, and still loved others.)
Yet I could not manage that task with *her*.
Is this the curse inherited from *first love?*
"Once bitten, twice shy", or so they often say...
Call me: thrice bitten, ne'er shy. In fact, make it,
Two hundred fifty times bitten, more like...
I'll never learn. Is my desired task impossible?
To ever leave all lost loves behind?
She is but one, if I really put mind to it,
Have I ever truly fallen out of love?
With anyone who I had once called "my love"?
In closing all the chapters of my past,
In fact, I think I threw the whole book out!
Yet my mind, refined to the grind,
So often reminds me of her kind.
Our time. As time unwinds, I can ne'er find,
An escape from any memory of *her*.

TADHG CULLEY

She stands for all of *them*, of that I'm sure,
They say, "Only unrequited love can be romantic".
I guess, still adding to this curse,
Since that potion, or the portion of my delusion,
Stirred ingredients into timely verse,
I cannot understand, (nor would I ever want to),
What keeps my essence tied to whate'er,
Has been left behind. What fate did weave,
Its course that found I could ne'er find a way,
To let *her* go...
This is something I suggest that I will never know.
It is the stuff that belongs to the Gods...
To know such mysteries is not a mortal task...
I've written films and songs and shows and plays,
And poems and fables, told at tables,
O'er which much wine and whisky spilled,
To numb (hide) tears that followed (dried),
With ink-stained hands that defy time,
What keeps me anchored at her shore,
No matter how far I sail away?
(...Is it the promises I wrote in love poetry!?)
What keeps my boat entangled, in a ceaseless sea-dance,
To her long-broken mast? What scuppers my maps,
Against the rocks of so many unseen shipwrecks?
That litter the coasts of their own natural hosts?
How can she still sow discord in my life,
From so far away, like an e'er singing siren?
With shrill-cry calls, always luring keel towards the crash?
This happens to the point where e'en memories of her,
Are now but lost and faded. Murky... Foggy at best.
She has all but evaporated from *my* view.
Still, I hear her Call on ancient airs; leading me to danger.
Is this experience the same for her, I wonder...
Am I alone in feeling this? Or does she feel this too?
Of such an answer, too, I will ne'er be shown.
Of that I'm almost certain. But hedge your bets...

Until the final curtain of my existence draws to close,
Still, I'll learn no answer, be none the wiser!
As to what causes two human souls,
To seek, meet, greet, *(fuck)*, fall in love,
To wreak the havoc that true heartbreak brings.
Where one person moves on so fast, so unaffected,
And yet the other soul moves on, pain-trailing,
Departing with all moments e'er lamented.
Ever affected by that long-lost *first love*...
As Muse descends to riddle/wrack my unwise mind,
Still my hand finds urgent need to write:
The musings of this broken-hearted life.
As if spilled ink can only dry when broken hearts bleed,
To share lifeforce with other souls who know such feelings?
Ever known, ever shown, finding homes with those in contact,
With such throes of dying romance. The embers of charred hearts.
I have been the boxer in the ring,
Who has come to know no stronger blow,
Than that which breaks the flooding heart!
The face and bones of broken nose will heal.
Where stitches serve to fasten skin, which dries the wound.
Yet I know no healing tactic for a broken heart.
There is no cure, no remedy, no vaccination,
Which can provide immunity to such a *fatal* pain.
That spends its future life force full-spent in vain.
It is as if such trauma is a vending machine,
Which I often return to, craving midnight snacks,
With coins in hand, whose trembling fingers, reaching out,
Dropping some, spilled into midnight streets,
Where neon lights provide just enough light to see,
The damned lost coin roll 'neath unreachable gaps!
Where neon lights provide just enough light to peer,
Through smeared, stained, dirty glass to find pain near,
As thumbs hungrily press, thirstily crunching numbers touched,
'Til candy snack that wracks my back will fall as food,
Tipping from the spool that kept it locked in place.

TADHG CULLEY

Now paid with price, crashing 'gainst glass,
Falling to dark pools where my thick hands and heavy heart,
Shall stoop, reaching in, through danger's darkness...
Searching for such cravings to be filled by cheapest snacks,
With blind eyes and sightless mind, fingers scraping vending tray,
Seeking nutrition-less nourishment:

Again and again,
Again and again,
And yet again,
And still again,
(And, why not, once more),

Begging to be filled by that which can never fill.
Devouring food from heartbreak's vending machine:

Over and over and over again.
Over and over and over again...
Over. And over. And over. Again.

'Til I can neither write nor breathe no more.

SHARDS OF A CERAMIC SOUL

'Forgive Me For Not Leaving'

Here I am,
Compelled to write,
Thought I'd retired,
From this life.

I took a break,
(Or so I thought),
To heal my mind,
And cure my soul.

Still, I find,
My mortal whole,
Can only write,
Delicacies of life.

So delicately,
At night-time hours,
While others sleep,
Drinking coffee at 3AM.

Writing in what,
Might as well be,
The *nine-hundredth* notebook,
That will be torn up.

Numbers seem,
Important to me,
Might be my,
Autistic tendencies.

While I count,
The published works,
The books, the poems,
The plays, the scripts...

TADHG CULLEY

The games, the radio,
The tv shows,
The many writings of my life,
Perhaps threefold have I destroyed.
(Maybe, in fact, make it tenfold)

I know the works,
That I destroy,
Number far more,
Than what remains.

Perhaps this is,
True metaphor,
Of my friendless,
Loveless life.
(Where all have been thrown away)

All my friendships are undone,
All my relationships ended,
I must, in fact, be brave,
To even carry on alone...

Been on rock bottom,
So many times, it feels like home,
The foundations of,
A thrice-bought throne.

Life is just,
Enduring suffering,
Learning how to not,
Count the many days, or many ways,
In which love is lost.

Life seems, to me, to be,
About forgetting,

And letting go,
Every wound and injury.

That ever caused us,
To fall or stumble,
Yet they still make us bleed...
And we can *seem* to crumble.

The greatest power,
I have found,
Or known, or shown,
Is not love... (Surprisingly)

To love feels easy,
It is so natural. Like falling off a cliff.
Gravity carries the job itself.
No... Not love... Love is a fool's task...
(Spent so unwisely)

To love is not to fight the current,
The heart will pump and flow it.
So, would you like to know,
My answer concerning said greatest power?

If you say yes,
Read one more line:

It's...

Forgiveness.

TADHG CULLEY

'I'll Tell You What It's Like To Lose Your Mind'

I'll tell you what it's like to lose your mind,
It's knowing, while you're alone in room,
Something else lurks within your chamber,
That overlooks each action of your mind.

It creeps along your skin, o'er each shoulder,
And tells you: "they are all coming to kill you",
You do not know the voice or where it comes from,
You do not know the "they" that are being spoken of.

Still your mind sees enemies in each shadow,
Every noise at night betrays their solemn vow,
To snuff out your soul, and spill your whole lifeblood,
Envisioning all the knives sent for your neck.

Each door that opens has that lurker behind,
Where every bare footstep falls onto glass,
Where every joke or laughter seems at your expense,
Where every living eye reports your location.

You'll hear the voices in the pipes of water,
The drip, drip tap will speak of your demise,
You'll hear an enemy in every branch sound,
Creaking outside with the silent breeze.

You'll sense demons encircling your safe-house,
You'll feel nature itself turn against you,
Perhaps you'll try to stem this pain with liquor,
Then bottle itself turns against you too.

You'll curse the Gods for trying to vanquish you,
You'll wonder who it was that cursed you so,
You'll see a snare in every meek adventure,
You'll sense failure seeking any help.

SHARDS OF A CERAMIC SOUL

Where everything seems to rise against you,
You see no way out but death at your own hand,
Just to stop this pain of mindset's oath-break,
I don't know how it stops when you've lost all.

I'll tell you what it's like to lose your mind,
(And still this forgets everything I know),
I've only tried to briefly describe,
The worst experience that I've ever known.

TADHG CULLEY

'Poetic Honesty'

I used to hate this style of modern poetry,
Forgive me, please, we all can change our minds,
It's all the mind seems capable to do,
Is change. And change. Still yet change some more.

This formless rhyme. This thoughtless flow,
That rolls; meanders to the place,
We cannot go, nor truly ever know.

…Where spacing is irregular.

Its meaning comes in currents,
(Mixed with currants in the reader's head),
Yet it arrives so splendidly,
Not whole (yet whole),
Ne'er finished (yet finished),
Straight from the heart,
And the mind,
And the soul,
Yet none of these places are where it truly comes from,
Some call it the subconscious,
Others claim it to be the stars,
To which some shaky stairs must reach our Muse,
Yet it pours with splendid spontaneity.
As if it catches author by surprise,
As well as all readers alike,
And if the words are not written down,
Some other lonely writer plucks them out,
From the sky,
From the ether,
Yet mine always feel mine.
Meant for me.
The beauty of such poetry.
Meant for you.

SHARDS OF A CERAMIC SOUL

I used to prefer the older, ancient style,
Of schooled and metered rhyming verse.
Rolling back the centuries,
To the shores on which they were written.
Whose songs sing timelessly through dusty verse,
I once despised that which now does grace my eyes,
My ears, my mind, my fingers, and my tongue.

(Such words and style that was born by Bukowski)

It's ironic since I've been that sort of reckless drunk.
Which sees poetic ramblings of a trauma's seed,
As something worth *devouring*,
Once or twice, or thrice, or countless times, have I,
Lost my mind to drugs,
Lost my heart to grief,
Lost my body to pain,
Lost my soul to life itself.

Perhaps Rejection is the Reason why,
I no longer give an actual fuck,
About critical review,
Or publisher opinion,
Or public chanting,
Or personal reason...

I am alive.
I have, many times, died,
And until that final moment,
(When I never return again)

I will write.

I will channel what comes to mind,
To record something of my life,
So I might leave something valuable behind.

TADHG CULLEY

I may ne'er learn long-lasting fame,
Or glory, nor success, nor earn real coin,
Or even hear others speak my name...

But my words might just touch:

Another's mind,
Another's heart,
Another's *soul*.

And if, for just one fleeting, tiny moment,
We are connected by one single thought,
And if, for just one fleeting, tiny moment,
That helps *you*...

...That would be enough.

SHARDS OF A CERAMIC SOUL

'Where Have I Been When I Was Gone?'

Where was I during my whole life?
When I was not quite fixed in body,
When I was not fastened to mind,
Who was the curator of my head?

As I view thirty-one whole years,
I cannot see the whole story,
Where one scene ends, unfolding,
Or when a chapter's truly closing…

I cannot think up a fancy title,
For full experience, confined,
I cannot sum up the messages,
That I might leave behind.

I cannot feel emotions,
That have long since passed and gone,
The tears, the blood, the heartache,
Are mere echoes in my ears.

You would have to *convince* me,
That I even came to Planet Earth,
Too many of my dreams have died,
Was I ever really, truly *here?*

The life I lead seems not my own,
I'm not so sure I have free will,
My future carved from past trauma,
That only served to make me ill.

The turbulence and suffering,
Of life's unsteady flight,
Brings me only cracks and shards,
That once were formed ceramic.

TADHG CULLEY

My kiln shattered long ago.
My pottery has gone to waste,
It seems I cannot even mould,
Wet clay with spinning haste.

I speak of feelings spent with tears,
But, in truth, I often find,
I'll only ever cry after,
One week waiting for 'em to come.

Hard feelings felt at back of throat,
I soon imprison them.
To cram them down into my gut,
While counting one-to-ten.

Then such volcanic fury,
Shows me I can ne'er escape,
From being alive; from being human,
Where lips taste salt-bound hate.

One week ago, that throat sensation,
Caused me to despair,
Knowing that, one week hence,
Ghost feelings come to share...

And then, at hours 'tween 3 and 4,
AM, will I but mourn,
Half-dreaming and in half-nightmare,
To wake, sheets soaked galore.

With pain in chest, it feels like dying,
Is this fatal heart attack?
I cannot find the breath for crying,
From forgotten emotion's blast!

If I calm down and recollect,
What brought such pain to surface,
I might blame PTSD,
Bi-polar, Autistic Spectrum.

OCD, Chronic Burnout,
Or any fancy term,
To but hide behind the fact,
That I am just a human.

Part of living is realizing,
We will one day die,
Part of that experience,
Is learning we're always parting…

Where each hello seems a goodbye,
And every journey's ending,
Ahead of curve, this fashion forms,
Before we know what's trending…

A life cannot even be viewed,
In hindsight. Since it's gone!
We can but murkily recollect,
False memories; a fiction spun.

They speak of "being present",
"Breathe in, that's it, breathe out",
But if life is only *breathing*,
Then I'd rather be a lung!

Being a human-being on Planet Earth
Seems such a paradox to me,
Since being the human that I've been,
My actions already seemed *done*.

TADHG CULLEY

If *I'm* not mind, body or heart,
Then *I* am in my soul,
And if I'm in what I can't *see*,
Can I ever be *known?*

Invisible realms so often seem,
So more real to me...
Since I am never present,
Yet feel a Destiny...

The past is gone, will future come?
If I am never here,
What matters? I've not left this room!
For years in exclusion.

Isolation of four years,
Weighed down my very soul,
I wonder if I'll ever be,
One day, once more, a *whole*.

Since I have come to Planet Earth,
'Cross these thirty-one years,
I've left so much of me behind,
I don't know what that leaves.

I used to know all that I was,
Thought I knew who I am,
But I was ever changing,
And rarely ever *one*.

Not one dream came true for me,
Trauma's grief was in the way,
I could not even focus,
On the days that I have seen.

Goodbye. When I ne'er said hello,
Farewell caught me off-guard,
Since I still feel wet behind ears,
Eyes still learning how to shed tears.

I've felt dead for so long a time,
I even wrote myself a sign:
It was only one simple line:
It simply read: "You are alive".

Goodbye. Goodbye. Goodbye. Bye-bye.
Guess it's time to go...
Then again, what do we ever,
Truly even know?

TADHG CULLEY

'Stolen Secrets Shared'

I've seen the heights of ecstasy,
I've viewed depths of despair,
I've known the sacred secrets,
That are locked inside our hair.

I've witnessed unseen mysteries,
Within ancestral lines,
I've decoded genetic histories,
Within rare bloodlines.

I've heard the silent whispers,
That are uttered by the stones,
I've felt gentle observations,
Of the age-old trees at home.

I've touched the bold resilience,
Of effervescent raindrops,
I've detected unlivable shock,
That sparked from lightning bolt.

I've learnt such hidden mysteries,
Of sight, sound, stone and bone,
Yet I could ne'er impart to you,
Knowledge of friendship's boon.

'A Note To Self'

I'm going to have to *just write*...
It's all I know how to do.
Write until I sell enough books to live.
Live until I sell enough books to write.
Get by until I can get by by writing.
Write 'til I can get by with what I get.
I've been broke, rejected, lost; traumatized,
So much that failure I should fear no longer!
I've had this inner voice in me since I was young.
When I was a kid, I knew my destiny.
When I wrote my first short story aged five.
I knew: "This is it. This sums up my life".
The World will know me one day for my writing,
I must wait for it to catch up to me,
I could think romantically and say,
"*To be a tortured artist is cliché,*
To be a struggling writer is the norm".
Therefore, I *must* be doing quite okay!

I've been doing this *properly* for 16 years,
I'd been doing it *wrong* for perhaps 11 more,
You know, I *might* be getting good at something,
When you only manage to "*get good*" at one or two...
Poetry sings from souls in most bleak hours,
When losing mind, I hear that voice inside,
Ask me what I want but what seems impossible,
It is to make a living writing poetry...
I am a humble Screenwriter by craft,
I aspire to be a Novelist by trade,
I've written many things 'cross 27 years,
But all of this serves me so that I can write...
<u>Poetry.</u>
Three years into my professional writing career,
It seems film and tv are now done with me!

TADHG CULLEY

For a decade I'd chased that broken dream,
Now back full circle where I left when starting!
Back into my barren hometown bedroom.
Dissolving into stark irrelevancy...
With nothing left to lose since I lost it all,
Time and time again and *then* some more...

Here I sit, insomniac bi-polar,
In the bedroom I moved into at 15,
Despite the 7 years I moved away,
I return at 31 where I began.
This fills me with false hope that all has *meaning*,
Meaning this room was where I was always *meant to be*,
I tried to chase my dreams *the right way*,
"Study hard, work hard, get your degree".
"Borrow money you don't have for education".
"Graduate, get shitty job; feign glee".

From broken home. Broke. Broken. What's left to break?
Except the bones that only mend themselves...
I sit with broken brain, so broken-hearted,
To remember, all I needed was a **PEN!**
Give me a journal, I'll fill it in three hours,
Give me a day, I'll magically live two,
See? I have only one single born talent,
That is to spill the ink that fills my heart.
I've reached a point in life where I can safely say:
"Fuck it *all*! I'm *taking* what I want!"
But I digress, let me turn back lost years,
Off I went to film school after grueling work,
On scholarship, (paying nothing), I couldn't afford,
Even rented roof over my head...
But a man will always somehow find money,
For drink and drugs no matter how empty his wallet...
When one's an addict or an alcoholic.
With shot in dark, I ruined Chance in fierce self-sabotage...

Somehow, (I know not how), I got that second degree,
To claim that I'm a Master of the Craft,
And now, returning home, I find,
That degree to be as useless as the first!
What I should have simply done *was this*:
(In fact, it's all that I am doing now,
In this short (long) journey aged 31),
It's Write, Write, Write, and then still Write some more,
Ignore critic, ne'er listen to jealous competition,
Let no-one else shepherd work nor your career,
You'll find the ignorant fill your head with lies,
Attempting to sabotage all that you had from birth,
Never listen to an envious critic,
Since they are twisted by their jealousy,
In fact, I find, leave all cold criticism,
To the kind that reads those blunt reviews…
When writing, there is but one task at hand,
That's write. Nothing more. That's it. Just write.
Anyone who tells you anything else.
Is trying to sell you something;
(Since they can't write-for-shit themselves!)

I won't yet bother to seek a publisher,
I've faced enough rejection by this point,
I couldn't even land elusive agent,
So, *fuck 'em all*, I'll do this by myself.
To be a writer one must only write.
I've dealt with unfair shares of disappointment,
So, in this age of free self-publishing,
I'll carve my own path doing it this way,
27 years spent writing, yet not creating product,
It took my suicide attempt 'fore I saw light,
In that moment, meeting (and greeting) Death,
I saved this unafraid desperation,
To attain all that I came to Earth to do…

TADHG CULLEY

No longer care for reception, nor the critic,
Must only express soul onto the paper,
Been far too long wasted, seeking acceptance,
Give up that rat race, to run your own.
Time to shed all plans, all hopes, all dreams;

Just go and get your important work done!

'Strawberry Milkshake'

The Berlin Wall came crashing down,
As I was torn from mother's womb.
Into an incubator thrust,
And yellow-stained, weak with jaundice.
So premature, two months too soon,
While struggling to breathe some more,
Umbilical cord wrapped 'round neck,
As if hangman's gallows were faced,
At birth; to dine on death. So slight,
Of frame, to fame of Caesar's name,
(The cut which tore from death to life),
Which gave baby "ceremony".

On that military barracks,
(Fitting place for Caesarian),
A life went on with car bomb scares,
And curtain threats with sniper's twitch,
To face a hate unknown yet felt,
So tangible in baby's room,
Where camo helms and uniforms,
Acted as a staged-set dressing,
Air raid sirens, all distressing,
Where Human-folk who breathed their last,
Would say "you ne'er see the bullet,
That steals your soul from mortal frame"...

A toddler of such childish games,
Will find imagination's ruse,
Can soon shift sorrow from the blues,
To elementary paint-splodge tunes,
Life goes on; keeps trucking on;
Where Disney cartoons forged the way,
On VHS tapes, counterfeit,
Taped o'er, borrowed, oh so shaky,

TADHG CULLEY

Managed to replicate the room,
In which light's dance illuminates,
Where Cinematic dream's wonder,
Flashed film forever for young eyes.

Yet a passion, forming pleasant,
Forged future torment to surpass,
Engraved upon a Prophet's diction,
Carved heartstrings which pluck for all nations,
Heavy heart inside chest beating,
Bearing soul to break through ribcage,
Brought the lines to mind where blue eyes,
Defied time; spoke of eternal.
Baby wrapped in second-hand clothes,
Silent... Melodic... Almost shamanic...
Carried weight of starstruck stances,
To defy heaven-sent chances.

Soon there was a father fleeing,
Medic-Soldier, (his brave cowardice,
Left solitary union,
Betraying his own wedding vows).
Soon there was a mother sitting,
Wondering what she might do,
To raise a child without a Dad,
"Sins of father" still pass on too,
Soon there was a son there sitting,
Forming a youth-wise mind-plight.
Soon there was a mother sitting,
Explaining where that Daddy went...

In this Germanic Motherland,
Despite British Forces invaded,
Saw this mum-and-son there roaming,
O'er flower-filled meadows, a bounty plenty:
Memories of bouncing baskets,

Tall ice-cream spoons and dinner plates,
Too many languages for so young a mind,
Where hearing mixed language made no sense!
German, French, Italian and English,
Were but few of what was heard here,
'Til this future poet's babbling burble,
Made up an unknown language of his own.

How to raise a child while being one being,
While doing job that really requires two?
Still it formed the soul-star shining,
Yet trauma was soon endured,
Still it sealed a prophet speaking,
For tradition to be ignored.
Oils were crossed on baby's forehead,
To a Catholic faith so foreign,
To Almighty God there pledged,
Before baby could digest food,
Set target for Legion's demons,
Such a sport for humans too…

The baby grew into a child,
Preferring animal company,
Than to mix with other children,
Found hearts of four-legged symmetry,
Dreamt such dreams veterinary,
Struggling with the chemistry,
Chanced hope's triumph in sporting life,
Yet moved into spheres artistic.
Destiny felt; calling, fated…
To leave the world a better place,
Not knowing where or how to start,
Lost to trauma, turmoil, torment.

TADHG CULLEY

Still a heart beats all the stronger,
Pounding on that doomed war-drum,
To a tune without banner,
To a field without champion.
To a sword without whetstone,
To a place without known name,
Ever searching, always roaming,
Since the sore soul sailed inside him.
Making mistakes 'til misshapen,
Lost without sole identity,
Knowing that there was destiny,
Ne'er knowing where that fate should lead.

Soon the childhood was there passing,
Unable to make sense of much,
Unable to "fit in" with others,
Learned solitary life,
Finding solace in the schoolwork,
Roaming 'round historical sites,
Moving back to ancient England,
Where Blood with Body reunites,
To true, loyal, small family,
Despite such heartache gathered 'round,
Found joy and warmth of hearth and home,
While drowning out unpleasant sounds.

There God-worship still continued,
Loving Christ 'neath candlelight,
Saying prayers each waking hour,
To a Catholic Primary sent,
To be taught God-fearing Creed,
Keeping naïve students quiet,
More obedient, to a fault,
Knowing they'll rebel one day,
Like immortal fallen angels,
Learning fates they will betray,

Speaking 'gainst what one day taught them,
To learn their wings were made of clay.

Still this young boy loved his Jesus,
Loved his Mum; grandparents too,
Loved his Uncles and his Aunties,
Finding adopted father true,
Filling vacant holes still gaping,
Teaching different worldly sights,
Briefly took that child to social,
Classes where he ne'er belonged.
Briefly seeing riches plenty,
Learnt nothing outlasts renting,
Losing access to those rare realms,
Losing Dad and mortgaged home.

Here the boy became a young man,
With a baby's unformed plan,
Too much heartache sent cascading,
Into devil's snare and can.
Here we find the Catholic roaming,
Target of so many souls,
Fiercer are those who go without,
(Those waiting for that Fall from Rome).
Here we see the thoughts now forming,
Of a teenaged mind hormone-filled,
To cast away all lessons taught,
And dare to tread life their "own way".

Here we hear the angels sighing,
Here we see the demons dancing,
Here we have the human falling,
Here we have the lessons learning.
Trip and stumble down a mountain,
Flying down to first view views,
Levitating e'er so dream-like,

TADHG CULLEY

Filling souls with horrors new.
Here we have the human burning,
Piled on crude coals, fanning flames,
Here we speak self-sabotage,
(Yet feel as though that's fated too!)

Down we go from Heav'n cascading,
Through clouds of Purgatory,
There we see the storms so molten,
With Hell-warning Destination.
Still we float up, not yet fallen,
Given chance anew with mercy,
Caught and captured at last hour,
From a nightmare we awaken,
Soon that vision, cold the brow,
Is a memory fading too,
Forgetting what chilled and burnt soul,
But remembering the stains of coal.

On we live, this frantic racket,
Into adulthood we broil.
Many more mature mistakes made,
To only earn predestined place.
Here we learn the path intentions,
(As good they are) *still* pave to Hell,
There we find the human pacing,
Cursing mortal dichotomy:
"Damned if you do, damned if you don't".
Whoever can form footsteps right?
Who can never dash their toe on,
Such rocks that fill this Planet Earth?

Human beings can earn such torment,
Despite ne'er leaving single room.
If their chances were formed perfect,
They'd find a way to ruin that too!

SHARDS OF A CERAMIC SOUL

How on Earth can any human,
Find true way through mortal life?
It seems to me the vital lessons,
Are only learnt by sheer mistake,
Every human biography,
Is filled to brim with chapters stark,
Where each passage, each page turning,
Seems to forebode a future dark.

Hence why, relying on God's mercy,
To forgive our many crimes,
No matter how small or little,
If given proper time to chime,
Or rhyme, or wit, what has been writ,
If given an eternity,
To judge ourselves, we'd find plenty,
Of reasons to condemn ourselves.
If could be granted e'erlasting vision,
We'd close our eyes and cry some more.
To see each action of our plays,
Played out for us, we'd close curtain.

I often wonder if we'll get,
A chance to review our own lives,
Retrospective 360* scope,
From ev'ry angle where we tangoed.
To see each thought or word or look,
Each action, every transaction,
From all points-of-view, would we,
Fall to dumbstruck insanity?
To see the ripple effects of,
Butterfly wings on oceans far,
That summon up a tsunami,
Unseen; to direst consequence.

Seems to me we're always fated,

TADHG CULLEY

To displease our True Creator,
How could we e'er please our Maker?
When mortal lives are so unbound?
Does this speak predestination?
Or into realms philosophy?
Seems to be the only duty,
Of true creative poetry...
Seems heaven-bound/hell-bound duty,
Depending on who is the Judge,
To ask questions mortals daren't ask,
To think we could e'er handle answers...

Yet we see this teenage manchild,
About to make one great foible,
To add another mistake made,
To the thousand-score on record,
Best to leave angelic stuff,
To the angels, since that's their work,
Best to leave work demonic,
To the demons, they're better suited!
Still angels and demons seem to,
Pester mankind at every turn,
To argue whispers from either shoulder,
Which choice to take at each dilemma?

Then the heart-shaped candle burning,
Casts shadows of their hearts on walls,
See elusive shapes flickering,
So momentary and ghost-like,
Almost reflecting, as wax simmers,
How fleeting romance seems from view.
Here we see two humans falling,
Into sheer chaos, that true love,
That one emotion which moves the world,
Away from war; division's cure,
Yet we have these teenage lovers,

About to break their hearts in two.

Take all romance of a lifetime,
And boil it down to just a few,
Here we write in cursive red notes,
On scented paper 'n envelopes,
Like the sticky substance nectar,
To seal the love she'll read in lieu,
Here we have the balloons popping,
With some confetti falling too...
This is where the dinner evenings,
Fill the calendar of seasons,
That seem to stretch eternally,
While disappearing far too soon...

First there was a summer romance,
Seemed undying, yet that died too,
Lips and fingers interlocking,
Where long-distance was tragic news,
Then we had some schoolyard flings,
After school and homework shirking,
Fans of sport and tentpoles climbing,
Road trips, mall dates, cinemas seats,
Many faces of youth's beauty,
Where youth is wasted on the young,
Heart cannot keep up with mindset,
Means these romances too soon flew.

Then we're off to University,
Where adult times are meant to shine,
Yet we find we're stumbling, drinking,
Tipsy, turvy, spin, drug-taking,
Hormones filling, raging through,
The bodies that we form anew,
Swimming bedsheets, swapping bed-sets,
Trying to squeeze in textbooks too,

TADHG CULLEY

Partying, clubbing, playing fields,
Mixing, speaking, listening; lost.

Dance concoction is too blurry,
To paint picture that could be viewed,
So, we'll leave it with some feelings,
That might better explain the truth,
Rollercoaster serenades,
In kaleidoscopic trance,
Where the ride becomes the rapids,
Before you even reach the top,
Dreams, ambitions, hopes and foibles,
Still lose yourself to form anew;
Rogue-like hormones and endorphins,
Mix cocktails that can ne'er be bought...

As soon as it began, it's over,
Heading home after three years,
Into work, forgetting soul plans,
Where memories cascade views,
Into work, forgetting soul dreams,
Where personality dulls and hides,
Into work, forgetting soul plot,
Where only turmoil can be found.
Into work, forgetting soul peace,
Plots its mental health breakdown,
More years pass by, while mixing lovers,
Desperate to find the Self it lost.

After nervous breakdown crisis,
After time, lost everything,
Rebuilding a base foundation,
From too many rock-bottom grounds,
Here we dare to flash smiles once more,
Here we share our heart kept treasure,
Here we pledge to ne'er forget the,

SHARDS OF A CERAMIC SOUL

True person we really are!
Shedding skin and social foreplay,
Casting out lessons we learned,
Ready to play Fool again,
Stepping blind-folded off the edge!

Here we learn that age means nothing,
Here we see, mid-twenties years,
Are just numbers, ever lying,
That only really speak of tears,
Here we dance with the immortal,
While ironically dying,
Yet we start to sense that something,
Plans each footstep we can't see.
Reminding ourselves of dreams,
We remember that we can live,
To learn what seems impossible,
Is what we so need to achieve!

Off to film school I went plodding,
On such a scholarship supreme,
Still, I was a broken man; being,
That which broken things can be...
Broken, breaking, breakdown-glee,
Chaos of passion, all confused,
Where dreams come true; so, we destroy 'em.
Just to feel oh so "in control".
Sometimes far scariest moments,
(When you get everything you want,
Where then you have it all to lose),
Mean you *relish* throwing it away.

Self-destructive catechisms,
Self-sabotage's cataclysms,
Only serve to tear down walls,
That you ironically built yourself,

TADHG CULLEY

False sense of self-preservation,
Only serve to keep out wolves,
That were already loose in your camp,
(Turned out to be set loose by *you*).
Where every gift and life's true blessing,
Is suspected as an enemy,
And paranoia's evil mind-seed,
Sets to ruin all you have.

It makes an enemy out of each friend,
Makes a demon out of every mate,
Makes betrayal so trustworthy,
A killing trap at every bait,
No fishing lines can e'er be trusted,
(Even when, in fact, a life vest),
Where lighthouses only lure in,
Ships to their own rock demise.
Now in professional life of writing,
All demons come for their prize,
Now barely a penny earning,
Learnt life is but to roll the dice…

Other Written Works by Tadhg Culley

Poetry Books – Available on Amazon
'Undo the Heartbreak' (Anthology of 150 poems)
'Unsung Lyricality' (Anthology of 68 poems)
'Relive the Romance' (Chapbook of 34 poems)
'Red Glows Only Lovers Know' (1 long poem)
'Melancholic Moments' (21 poems)

Novellas – Available on Amazon
'The Poet And The Prostitute'
'The Holler Screams'
'Gridlock Deadlock'

Short Story Collection – Available on Amazon
'Secrets Buried In The Woods'

Memoir – Available on Amazon
'Paperback Silverback'

Feature Film Screenplays
'Endless Life' (Realist Drama)
'Cold Star' (Gritty Drama)
'Stepping Stones' (Thriller/Horror)
'Tailback' (Thriller)
'Urbex' (Thriller)
'Quarrying Souls' (Supernatural Horror)
'The Long Barrow' (Archaeological Horror)
'Mouth of the Hollow' (Revenge Thriller)
'Our Love Shook The Berlin Wall' (Romance Thriller)
'In Cinemas Now' (Supernatural Horror)

TV Series Screenplays
'Death Duty' (Supernatural Horror)
'Wardens' (Sit Com)

About the Author

Tadhg Culley is a Professional Screenwriter, Published Author and Poet from the UK. He has written ten feature film screenplays, eight TV series scripts, six poetry books, three novellas, three guidebooks, one memoir, one collection of short stories, and many other short-form works, delving into documentary, theatre, animation and games. He is a BAFTA Scholar and graduate of both the National Film & TV School (NFTS) & the University of Creative Arts (UCA).

Printed in Great Britain
by Amazon